LAUGH-OUT-LOUD JOKES

LAUGH-OUT-LOUD HOLIDAY JOKES

CAITIE MCANENEY

WINDMILL BOOKS

Published in 2025 by Windmill Books, an Imprint of Rosen Publishing
2544 Clinton St., Buffalo, NY 14224

First Edition

Editor: Caitie McAnene
Book Design: Claire Zimmermann

Photo Credits: Cover, p.1 (child laughing) Lopolo/Shutterstock.com; series art (illustrations) Nadzin/Shutterstock.com, (paper texture) OanaGherghe2/Shutterstock.com; p. 5 Evgeny Atamanenko/Shutterstock.com; p. 7 Shutterstock AI Generator/Shutterstock.com; p. 9 masterpiece creator/Shutterstock.com; p. 11 Pixel-Shot/Shutterstock.com; p. 13 Jose Luis Carrascosa/Shutterstock.com; p. 15 gpointstudio/Shutterstock.com; p. 17 Andrii Spy_k/Shutterstock.com; p. 19 Heather A. Craig/Shutterstock.com; p. 21 PeopleImages.com - Yuri A/Shutterstock.com.

Library of Congress Cataloging-in-Publication Data

Names: McAneney, Caitie, author.
Title: Laugh-out-loud holiday jokes / Caitie McAneney.
Description: Buffalo, NY : Windmill Books, 2025. | Series: Laugh-out-loud jokes | Includes index.
Identifiers: LCCN 2024009268 (print) | LCCN 2024009269 (ebook) | ISBN 9781538396896 (library binding) | ISBN 9781538396889 (paperback) | ISBN 9781538396902 (ebook)
Subjects: LCSH: Holidays–Juvenile humor. | Wit and humor, Juvenile. | LCGFT: Humor.
Classification: LCC PN6231.H547 M33 2024 (print) | LCC PN6231.H547 (ebook) | DDC 808.87/9334–dc23/eng/20240312
LC record available at https://lccn.loc.gov/2024009268
LC ebook record available at https://lccn.loc.gov/2024009269

Manufactured in the United States of America

CPSIA Compliance Information: Batch #CSWM25. For further information, contact Rosen Publishing at 1-800-237-9932

CONTENTS

Words in the glossary appear in **bold** the first time they are used in the text.

CHRISTMAS CHEER

What do you call a cat who spends Christmas on the beach?

SANDY CLAWS.

What's Frosty the Snowman's favorite cereal?

SNOWFLAKES.

What do sheep say when you wish them a Merry Christmas?

BAAA-HUMBUG!

What do Santa's helpers learn in school?

THE ELFABET.

FUN FACT!

"Bah! Humbug!" is a famous phrase used by Ebenezer Scrooge, the grumpy main character in *A Christmas Carol* (1843).

FUNNY VALENTINE

How do farmers celebrate Valentine's Day?

WITH LOTS OF HOGS AND KISSES.

What did the orca say to his crush on Valentine's Day?

"WHALE YOU BE MINE?"

What did one shoe say to the other on Valentine's Day?

"YOU'RE MY SOLE-MATE."

Why do skunks celebrate Valentine's Day?

THEY'RE SO SCENT-IMENTAL.

FUN FACT!

Valentine's Day is a holiday celebrated on February 14 in which people give **sentimental** cards and gifts to **express** their love.

SILLY ST. PATRICK'S DAY

Why did the leprechaun have to borrow money?

BECAUSE HE WAS A LITTLE SHORT.

What's a leprechaun's favorite kind of music?

SHAM-ROCK.

What do you get when you cross a leprechaun and a vegetable?

LEPRE-CORN.

Why did the leprechaun go to the furniture store?

TO BUY A SHAMROCKING CHAIR.

FUN FACT!

According to Irish **folklore**, leprechauns are fairies in the form of tiny, bearded men.

HOPPY EASTER

Why was the Easter egg hiding?

IT WAS A LITTLE CHICKEN!

Where did the rabbits go after they got married?

ON THEIR BUNNYMOON.

Where did the vampire keep her Easter eggs?

IN HER EASTER CASKET.

How does the Easter Bunny travel?

ON A HAREPLANE.

FUN FACT!

Baby bunnies and chicks are often **associated** with Easter because this Christian holiday falls in springtime—a time of new life.

LIBERTY AND LAUGHS

What did the ghost wear for the Fourth of July?

RED, WHITE, AND BOO.

Does everyone have off from work on Independence Day?

NO, FIRE WORKS.

What's a duck's favorite thing to play with on Independence Day?

FIRE-QUACKERS.

Why are there no knock-knock jokes about the United States?

BECAUSE FREEDOM RINGS.

FUN FACT!

The Declaration of Independence has a date of July 4, 1776. However, it wasn't signed until August 2, 1776.

HALLOWEEN HUMOR

Who likes to trick people on Halloween?

PRANK-ENSTEIN.

Why didn't the skeleton go out for Halloween?

HE DIDN'T HAVE THE GUTS.

What do witches learn in school?

SPELLING!

Where do baby monsters go during the day?

DAY-SCARE.

FUN FACT!

Frankenstein was a novel written by Mary Shelley in 1818. In the story, Frankenstein is a scientist—not the monster, as he is often **portrayed.**

BOO TO YOU!

What did one ghost say to another?

"GET A LIFE!"

Who sells cookies to ghosts?

GHOUL SCOUTS.

What's a ghost's favorite dessert?

I SCREAM.

Why couldn't the ghost lie?

BECAUSE YOU COULD SEE RIGHT THROUGH HIM.

FUN FACT!

About 40 percent of Americans believe in ghosts.

THANKSGIVING TREATS

Why do turkeys love the rain?

IT'S FOWL WEATHER.

What did the turkey say at Thanksgiving dinner?

"GOBBLE UP, EVERYONE."

What instrument did the turkey bring to dinner?

A DRUMSTICK.

What sport do pumpkins play?

SQUASH.

FUN FACT!

In 1621, dozens of English settlers and Wampanoag people gathered in today's Massachusetts for a feast to celebrate a successful **harvest**.

BIRTHDAY BITS

How did the mermaid spend her birthday?

SHE HAD A SHELLEBRATION.

What kind of music do birthday balloons hate?

POP.

Why didn't the teddy bear want his birthday cake?

HE WAS STUFFED.

What did one sheep say to the other on her birthday?

"HAPPY BIRTHDAY TO EWE."

FUN FACT!

The most common birthday in the United States is September 9.

GLOSSARY

associate: To connect one thing to another thing your mind.

casket: A box in which a dead person is buried.

ewe: An adult female sheep.

express: To make thoughts or feelings known by saying or writing.

folklore: The stories and ways of a group of people from a certain place or country that are handed down through the years.

fowl: A bird that is raised for its eggs or meat.

ghoul: An evil spirit that is believed to eat people and dead bodies.

harvest: The gathering of ripe crops, or the amount gathered.

portray: To make a picture of someone or something in images or words.

sentimental: Causing or showing tender feelings.

FOR MORE INFORMATION

BOOKS

Brundle, Joanna. *Celebrations Around the World.* Minneapolis, MN: Jump!, Inc., 2024.

Felix, Rebecca. *Mini Holiday Crafts to Celebrate in Style.* North Mankato, MN: Capstone Press, 2024.

Morgan, Elizabeth. *Celebrating Christmas.* New York, NY: Cavendish Square Publishing, 2023.

WEBSITES

The First Thanksgiving
kids.nationalgeographic.com/history/article/first-thanksgiving
Read more about the first Thanksgiving with National Geographic Kids.

Weird but True!: Halloween
kids.nationalgeographic.com/weird-but-true/article/halloween-1
Enjoy more fun facts about Halloween.

Publisher's note to educators and parents: Our editors have carefully reviewed these websites to ensure that they are suitable for students. Many websites change frequently, however, and we cannot guarantee that a site's future contents will continue to meet our high standards of quality and educational value. Be advised that students should be closely supervised whenever they access the internet.

INDEX